FIVE 5 FINGER
PIANO

PRAISE & WORSHIP

T0058922

CONTENTS

2 awesome god

7 how majestic is your name

10 lord, be glorified

14 praise the name of jesus

11 lord, i lift your name on high

16 shine, jesus, shine

19 step by step

22 there is a redeemer

ISBN 0-634-06692-7

HAL•LEONARD®
CORPORATION

7777 W. BLUEMOUND RD. P.O. BOX 13819 MILWAUKEE, WI 53213

For all works contained herein:
Unauthorized copying, arranging, adapting, recording or public performance is an infringement of copyright.
Infringers are liable under the law.

Visit Hal Leonard Online at
www.halleonard.com

Awesome God

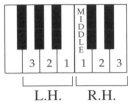

L.H.   R.H.

Words and Music by
Rich Mullins

Moderately

When He | rolls up His sleeve, He ain't just | "Put - tin' on the Ritz." Our
sky | was star - less in the | void of the night, our

God is an awe - some God! There is
God is an awe - some God! He spoke

Duet Part (Student plays one octave higher than written.)

Moderately

Copyright © 1988 by BMG Songs, Inc.
International Copyright Secured   All Rights Reserved

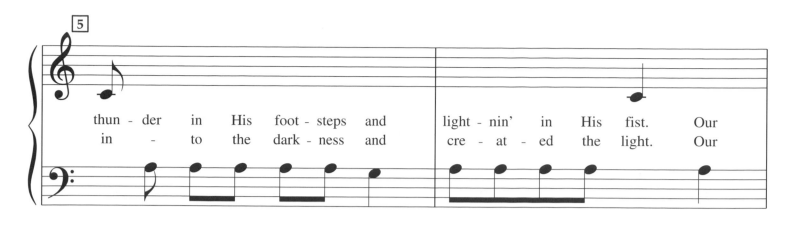

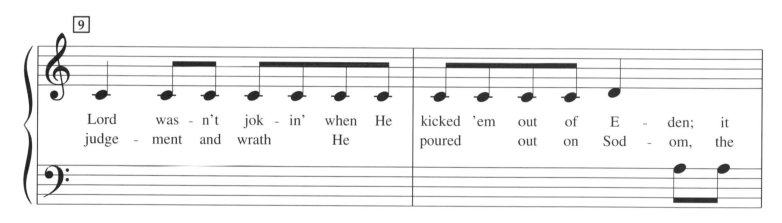

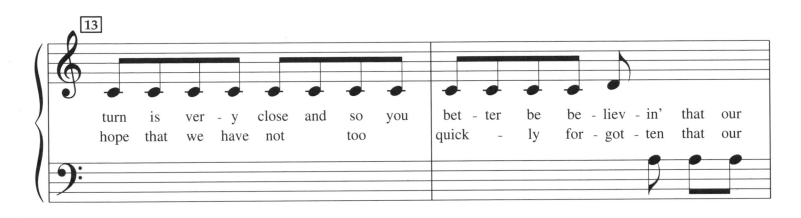

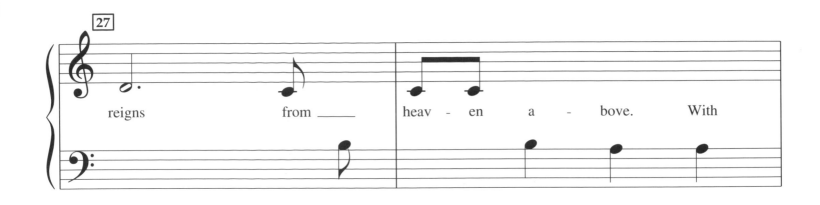

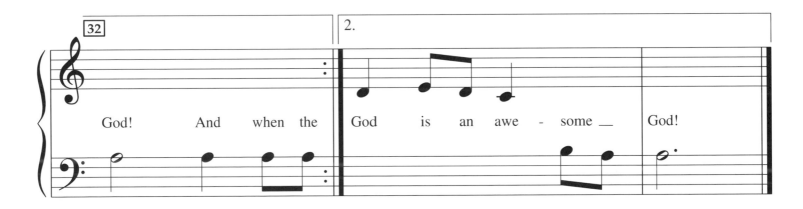

How Majestic Is Your Name

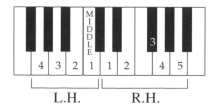

Words and Music by
Michael W. Smith

Duet Part (Student plays one octave higher than written.)

© 1981 MEADOWGREEN MUSIC COMPANY
Admin. by EMI CHRISTIAN MUSIC PUBLISHING
All Rights Reserved   Used by Permission

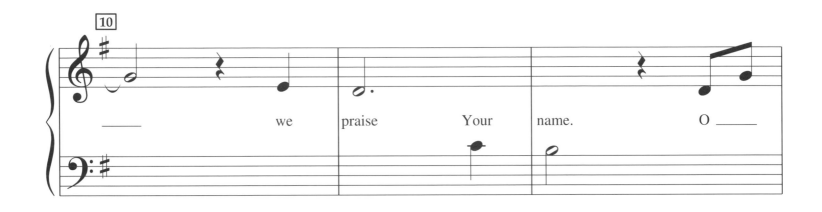

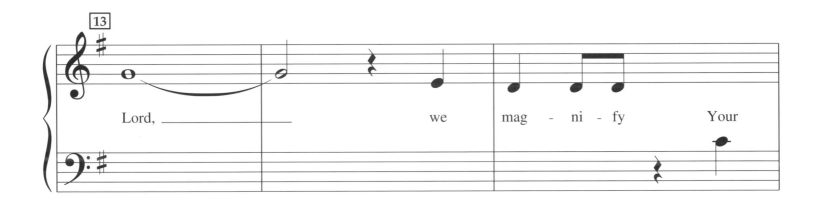

name, ___ Prince of Peace, ___ Might - y God, O ___

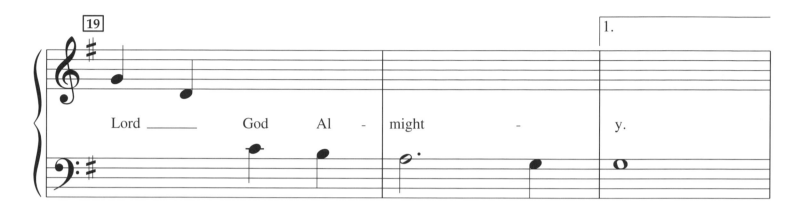

Lord ___ God Al - might - y.

1.

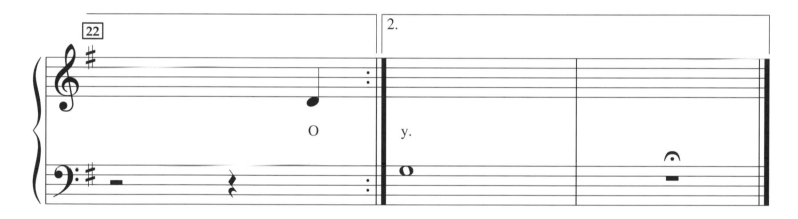

2.

O y.

Lord, Be Glorified

L.H.   R.H.

Words and Music by
Bob Kilpatrick

Moderately

1. In my life, Lord, be glo-ri-fied, be glo-ri-fied.
2., 3. *(See additional lyrics)*

In my life, Lord, be glo-ri-fied to-day.   day.

Additional Lyrics

2. In my song. . .

3. In Your church. . .

Duet Part (Student plays one octave higher than written.)

Moderately

© 1978 by Bob Kilpatrick Music
Assigned 1998 to Lorenz Publishing Co.
All Rights Reserved   International Copyright Secured   Used by Permission

Lord, I Lift Your Name on High

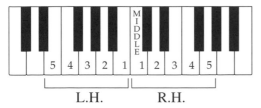

L.H.   R.H.

Words and Music by
Rick Founds

Moderately

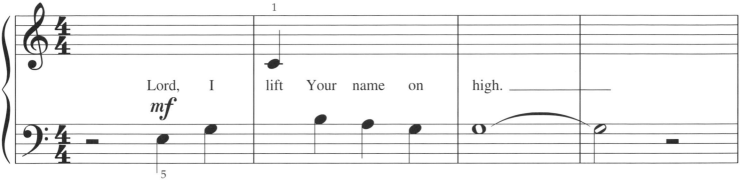

Lord, I lift Your name on high. _____

mf

Lord, I love to sing Your prais - es. _____

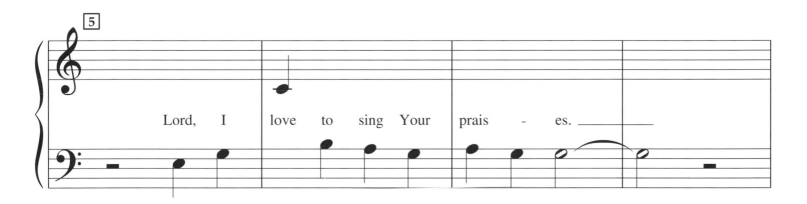

Duet Part (Student plays one octave higher than written.)

Moderately

mf

© 1989 MARANATHA PRAISE, INC. (Administered by THE COPYRIGHT COMPANY, Nashville, TN)
All Rights Reserved   International Copyright Secured   Used by Permission

way, from the earth ___ to the cross my debt to

pay. From the cross ___ to the grave, from the grave ___ to the

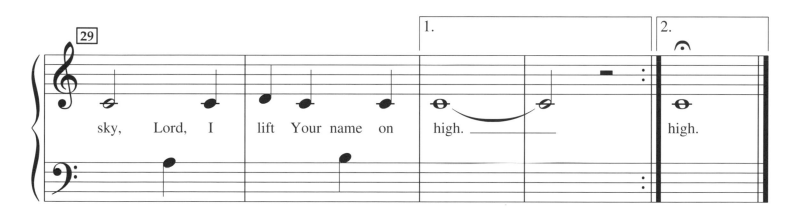

1.

sky, Lord, I lift Your name on high. ___ high.

2.

Praise the Name of Jesus

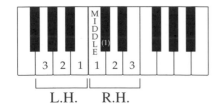

Words and Music by
Roy Hicks, Jr.

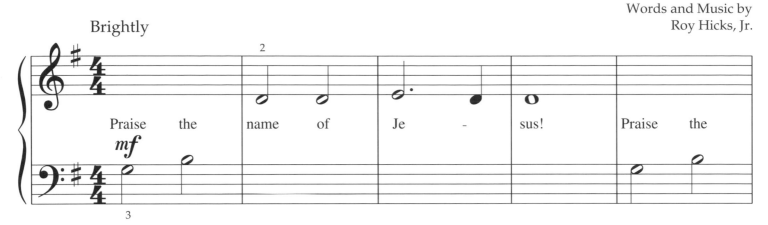

Brightly

Praise the name of Je - sus! Praise the

name of Je - sus! He's my Rock,

Duet Part (Student plays one octave higher than written.)

Brightly

© 1976 LATTER RAIN MUSIC
Admin. by EMI CHRISTIAN MUSIC PUBLISHING
All Rights Reserved   Used by Permission

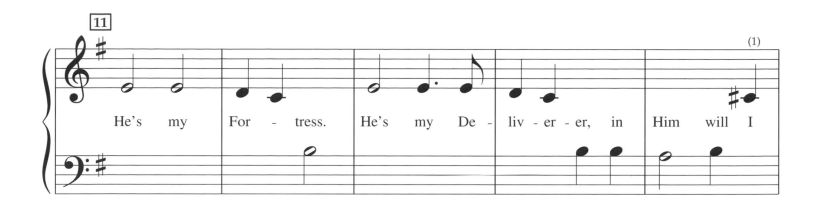

He's my For - tress. He's my De - liv - er - er, in Him will I

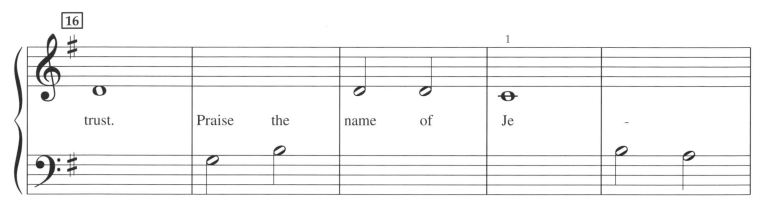

trust. Praise the name of Je -

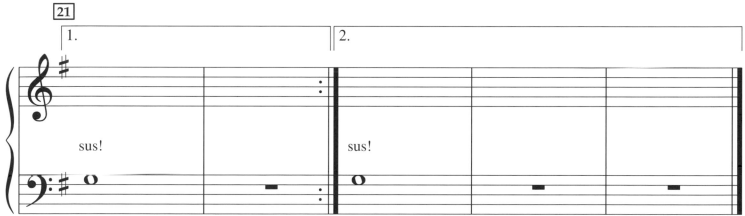

sus!   sus!

Shine, Jesus, Shine

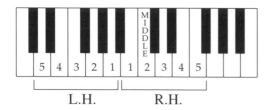

Words and Music by
Graham Kendrick

With excitement

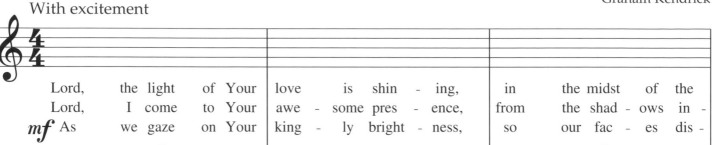

Lord,   the light   of Your   love   is   shin - ing,   in   the midst   of the
Lord,   I come   to Your   awe - some pres - ence,   from   the shad - ows in - to
mf As   we gaze   on Your   king - ly   bright - ness,   so   our fac - es dis -

dark - ness shin - ing.   Je - sus, Light   of the   world shine up - on ___ us,
to   Your ra - diance.   By   the blood I may   en - ter Your bright - ness;
play   Your like - ness.   Ev - er   chang - ing from   glo - ry   to   glo - ry,

Duet Part (Student plays one octave higher than written.)

With excitement

© 1987 Make Way Music (admin. by Music Services in the Western Hemisphere) (ASCAP)
All Rights Reserved   Used by Permission

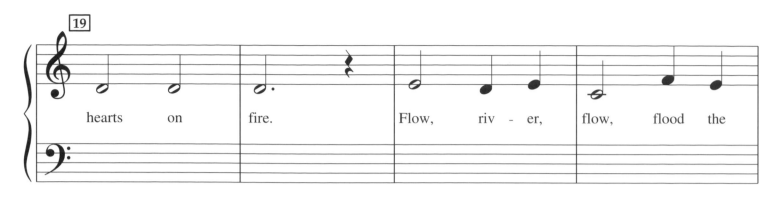

hearts on fire. Flow, riv - er, flow, flood the

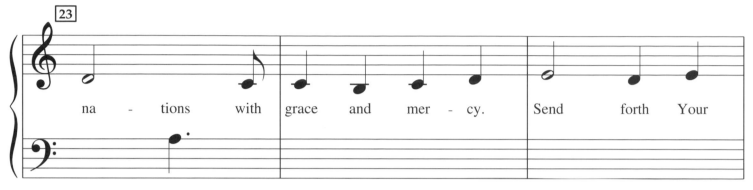

na - tions with grace and mer - cy. Send forth Your

Word, Lord, and let there be light. light.

Step by Step

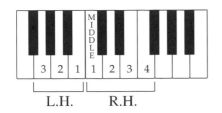

L.H.   R.H.

Words and Music by
David Strasser "Beaker"

Moderately fast

O God, You are my ___ God, and I will ev-er praise ___

you. O God, You are my ___ God and

Duet Part (Student plays one octave higher than written.)

Moderately fast

Copyright © 1991 by BMG Songs, Inc. and Kid Brothers Of St. Frank Publishing
All Rights Administered by BMG Songs, Inc.
International Copyright Secured   All Rights Reserved

There Is a Redeemer

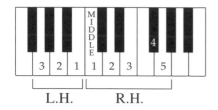

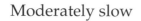

Words and Music by
Melody Green

Moderately slow

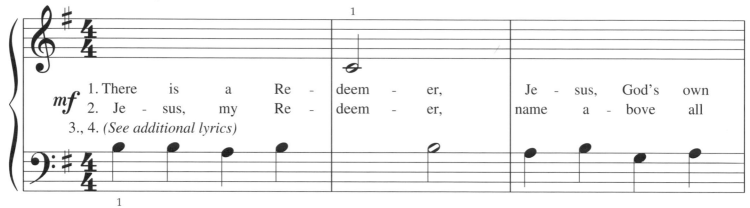

1. There is a Re - deem - er, Je - sus, God's own Son.
2. Je - sus, my Re - deem - er, name a - bove all names.
3., 4. *(See additional lyrics)*

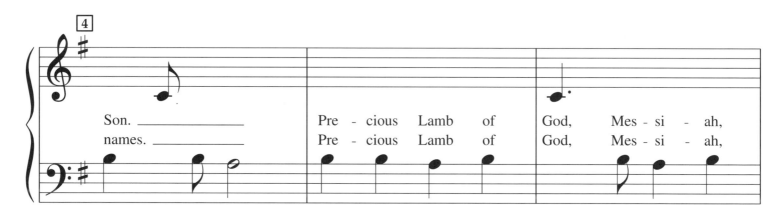

Son. _____ Pre - cious Lamb of God, Mes - si - ah,
names. _____ Pre - cious Lamb of God, Mes - si - ah,

Duet Part (Student plays one octave higher than written.)

Moderately slow

© 1982 BIRDWING MUSIC, BMG SONGS, INC. and EARS TO HEAR MUSIC
Admin. by EMI CHRISTIAN MUSIC PUBLISHING
All Rights Reserved   Used by Permission

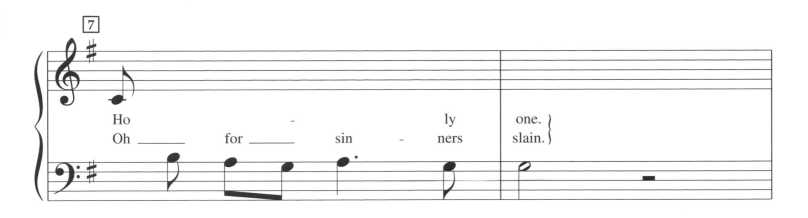

Ho - ly one. }
Oh _____ for _____ sin - ners slain. }

9 **Chorus**

Thank You, oh my Fa - ther, for giv - ing us Your

12

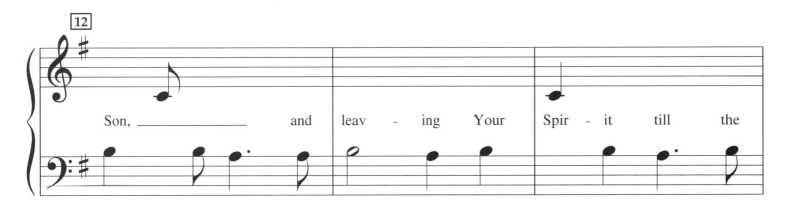

Son, _____ and leav - ing Your Spir - it till the

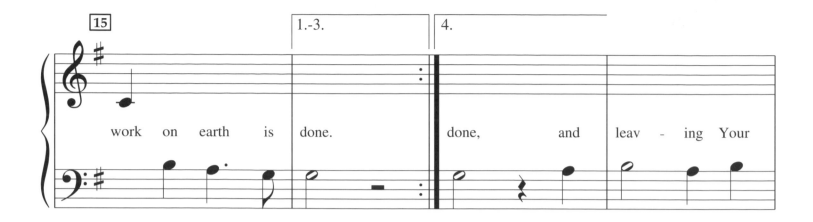

Additional Lyrics

3. When I stand in glory, I will see His face.
   And there I'll serve my King forever in that holy place.
   Chorus

4. There is a Redeemer, Jesus, God's own Son.
   Precious Lamb of God, Messiah, Holy One.
   Chorus